AUTHENTIC TRANSCRIPTIONS
WITH NOTES AND TABLATURE

Ray La Montagne   Gossip In The Grain

T0079953

Music transcriptions by Pete Billmann

ISBN 978-1-4234-6902-5

7777 W. BLUEMOUND RD. P.O. BOX 13819 MILWAUKEE, WI 53213

Visit Hal Leonard Online at
www.halleonard.com

You Are the Best Thing

Words and Music by Ray LaMontagne

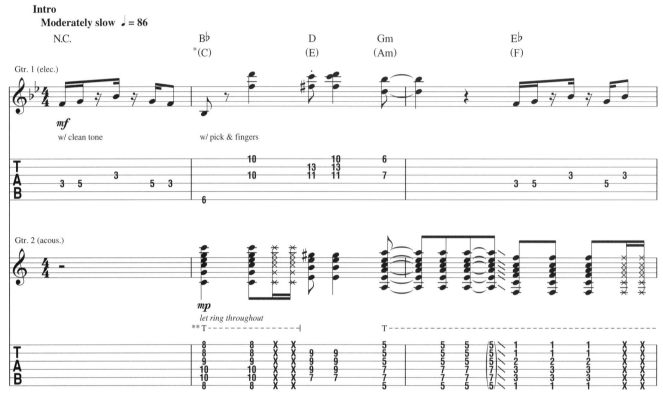

Gtr. 2: Tune down 1 step:
(low to high) D-G-C-F-A-D

Intro

Moderately slow ♩ = 86

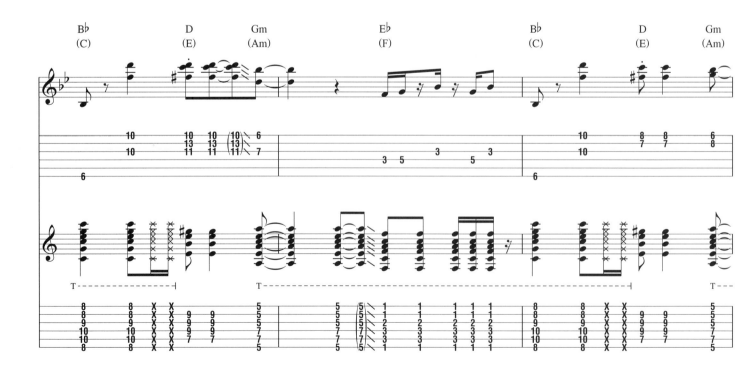

*Symbols in parentheses represent chord names respective to detuned guitar.
Symbols above reflect actual sounding chords.

**T = Thumb on 6th string

To Coda 1 ⊕

4

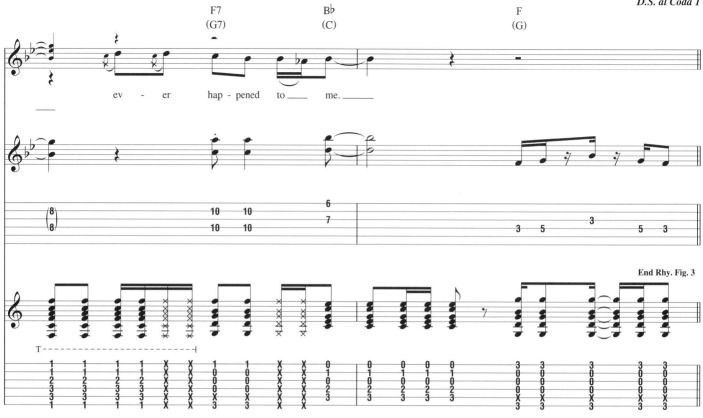

D.S. al Coda 1

Coda 1

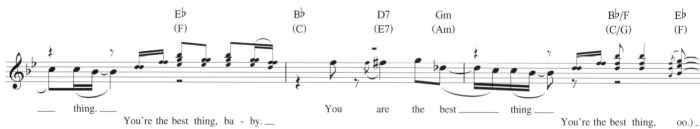

To Coda 2

Outro-Chorus

Let It Be Me

Words and Music by Ray LaMontagne

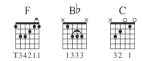

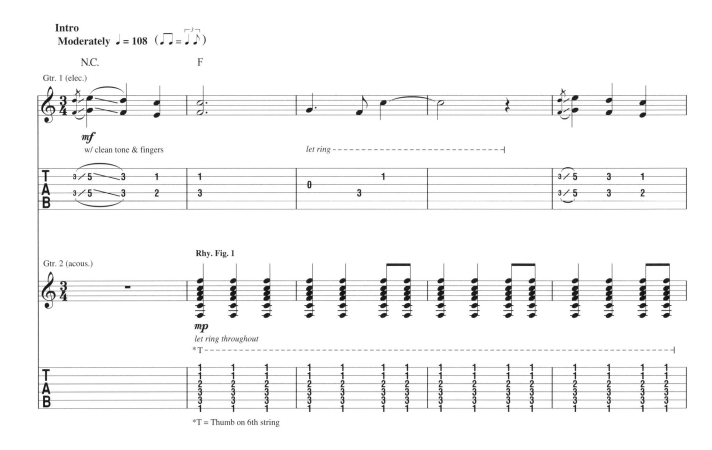

*T = Thumb on 6th string

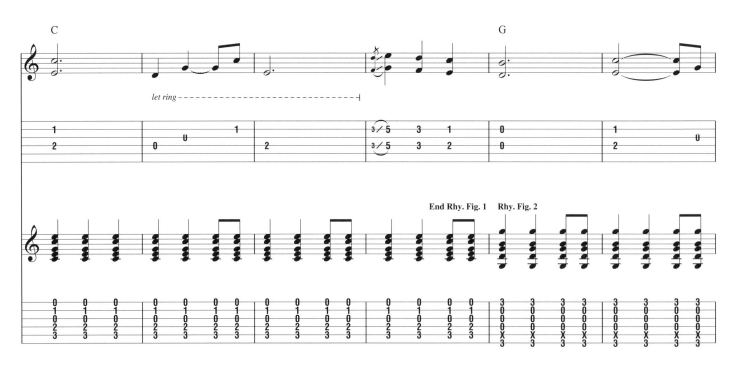

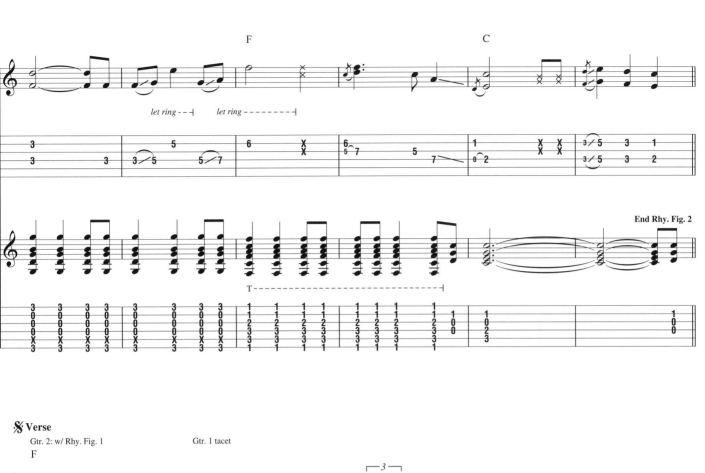

End Rhy. Fig. 2

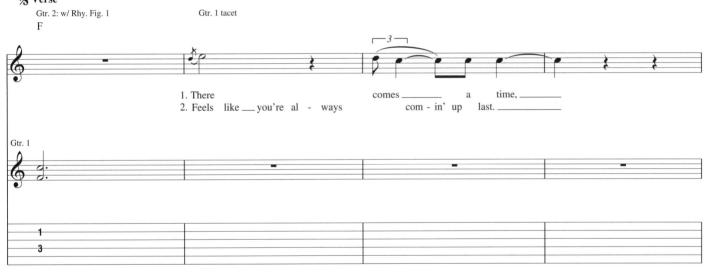

% Verse

Gtr. 2: w/ Rhy. Fig. 1

Gtr. 1 tacet

F

1. There   comes _____ a time, _____
2. Feels like __ you're al - ways com - in' up last. _____

Gtr. 1

C

a time   in ev - 'ry - one's _ life _____
Pock - ets full of noth - ing, ain't got _ no _ cash. _____

Gtr. 2: w/ Rhy. Fig. 2 (1st 4 meas.)

G

when noth - ing seems _ to go your way, _____
No _____ mat - ter where you turn, _ you ain't got no place to stand, _ yeah.

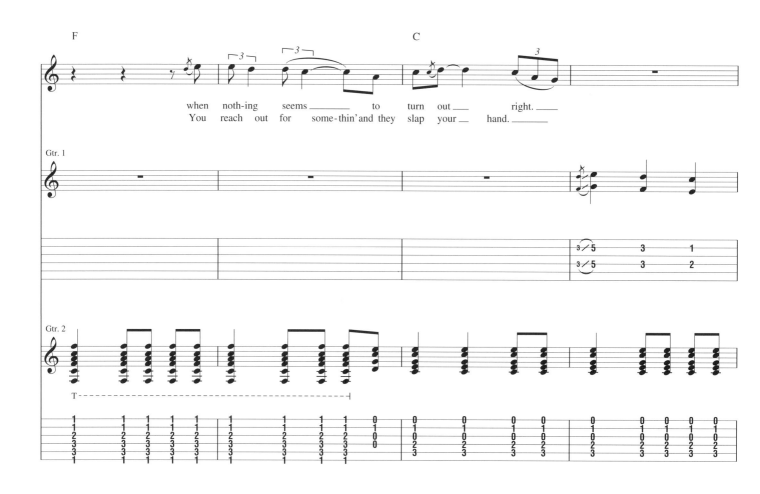

when noth-ing seems _____ to turn out ___ right. _____
You reach out for some-thin' and they slap your ___ hand. _____

Gtr. 1

Gtr. 2

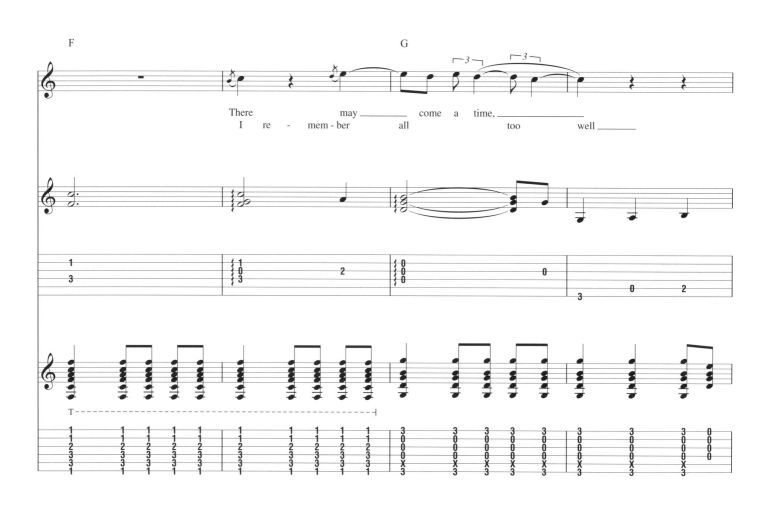

There may _____ come a time, _____
I re - mem - ber all _____ too well _____

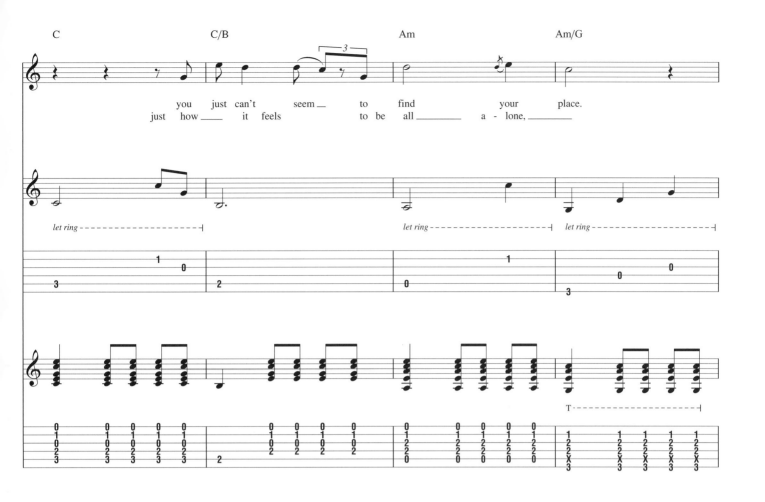

you just can't seem __ to find your place.
just how __ it feels to be all __ a - lone, __

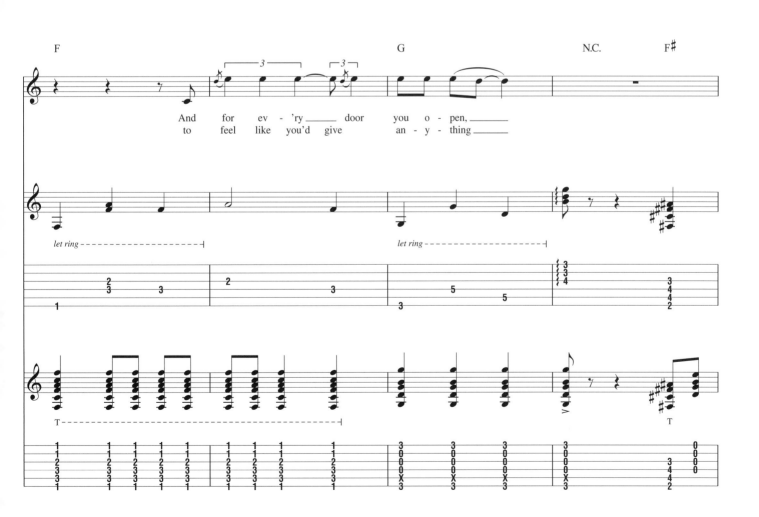

And for ev - 'ry __ door you o - pen, __
to feel like you'd give an - y - thing __

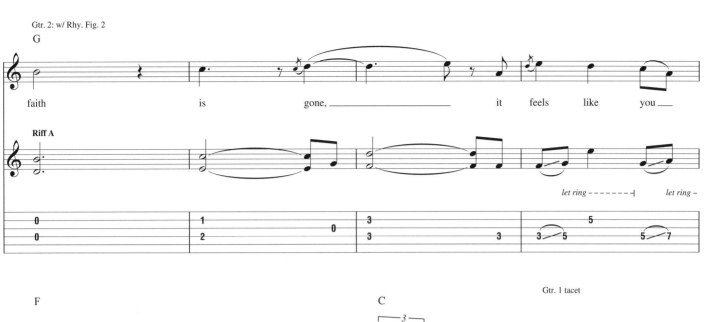

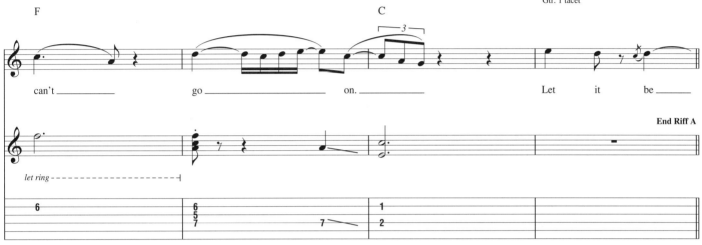

Chorus

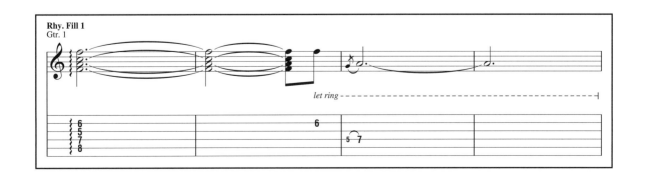

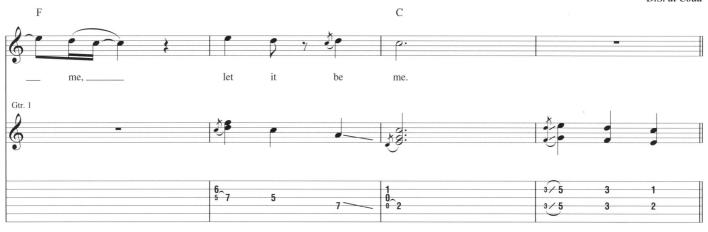

F — me, — let it be me.   C

Gtr. 1

⊕ Coda

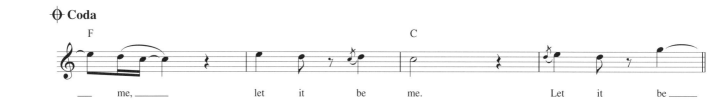

F — me, — let it be me.   C   Let it be —

Outro-Chorus

Gtr. 2: w/ Rhy. Fig. 1

F — me, — let it be me. —

Gtr. 2: w/ Rhy. Fig. 2 (1st 4 meas.)

G   If it's a friend you need, — let it be

F me, — G let it be — me, — let it be — me.   C

Gtr. 1

Gtr. 2

Sarah

Words and Music by Ray LaMontagne

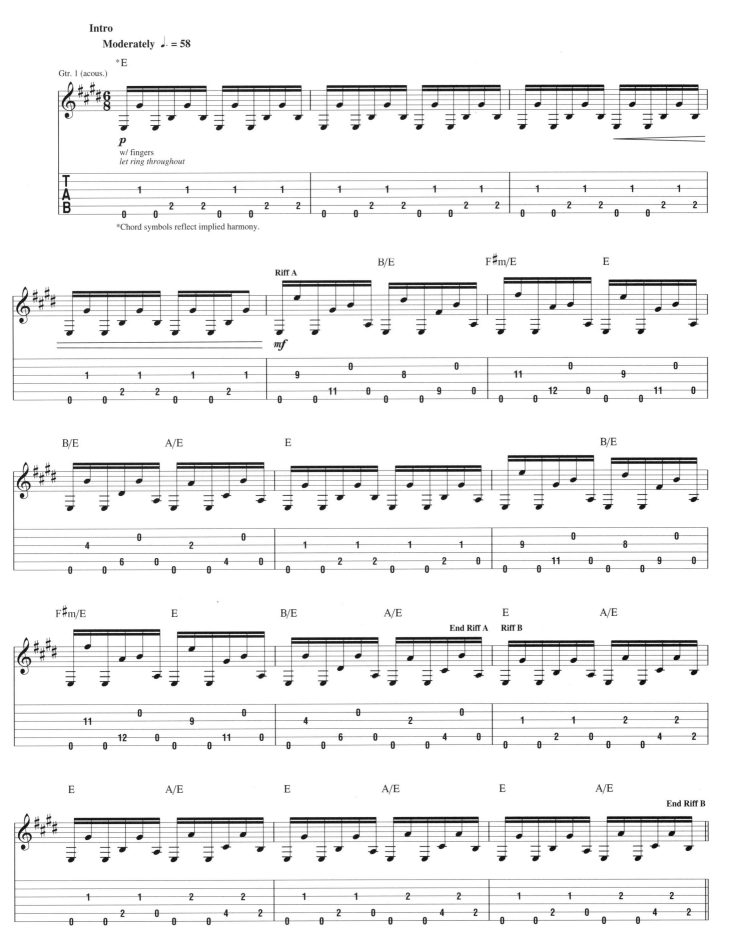

Interlude

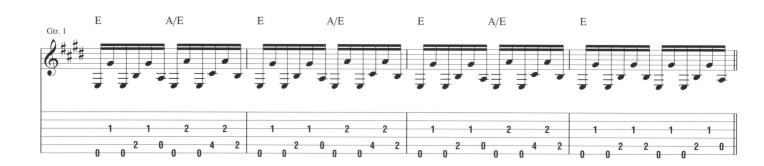

Bridge

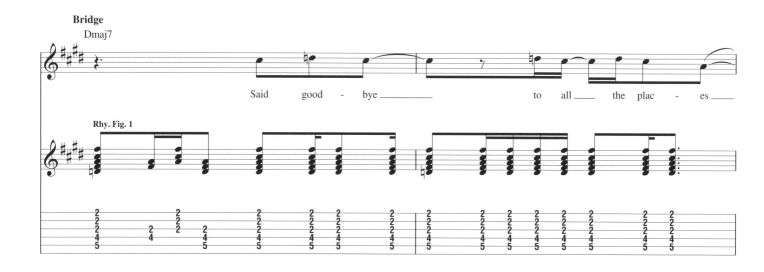

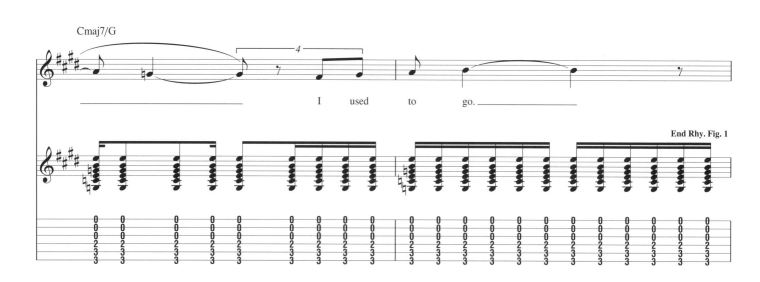

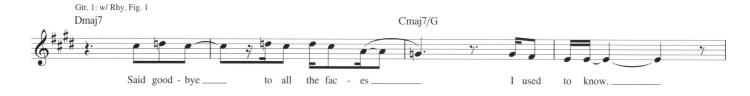

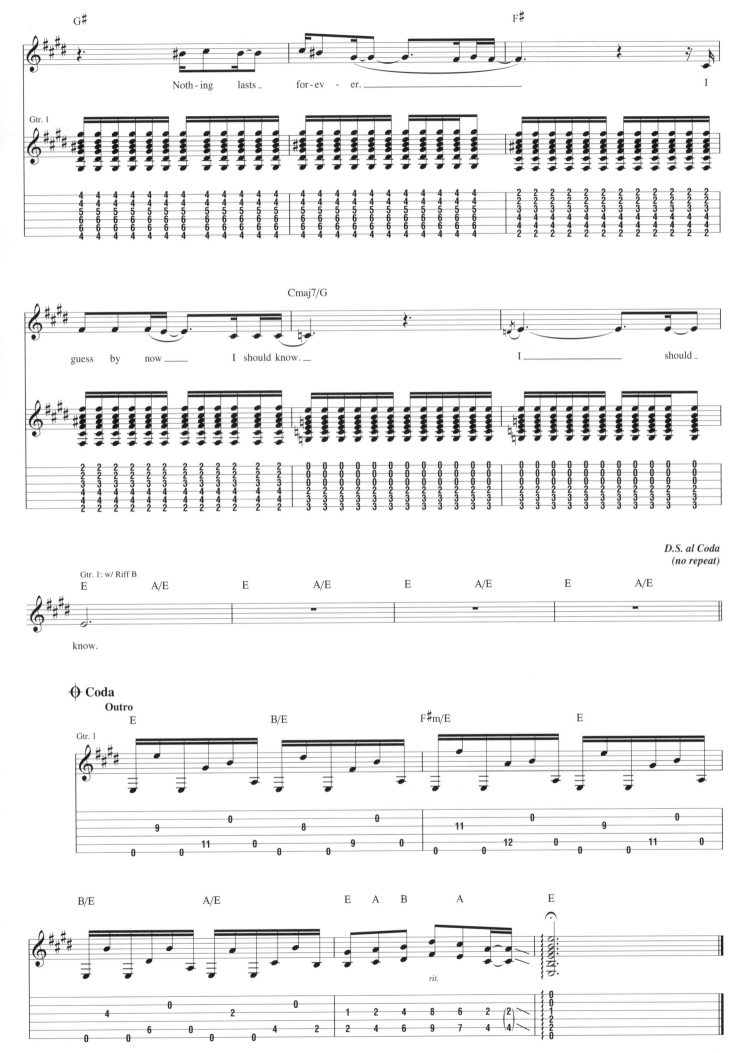

I Still Care for You

Words and Music by Ray LaMontagne

Tune down 1 step:
(low to high) D-G-C-F-A-D

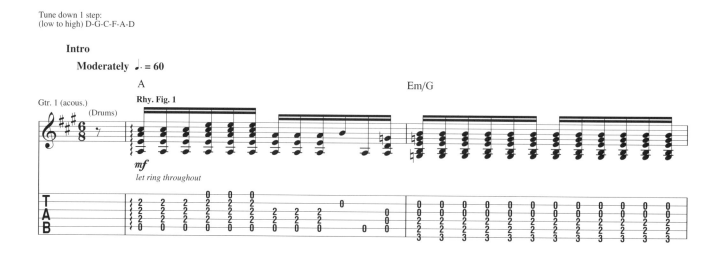

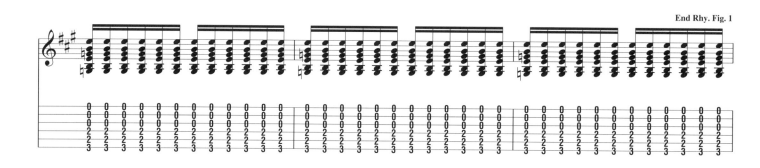

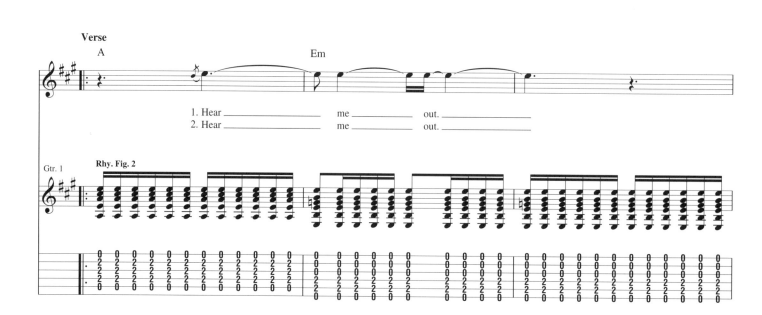

1. Hear _____ me _____ out. _____
2. Hear _____ me _____ out. _____

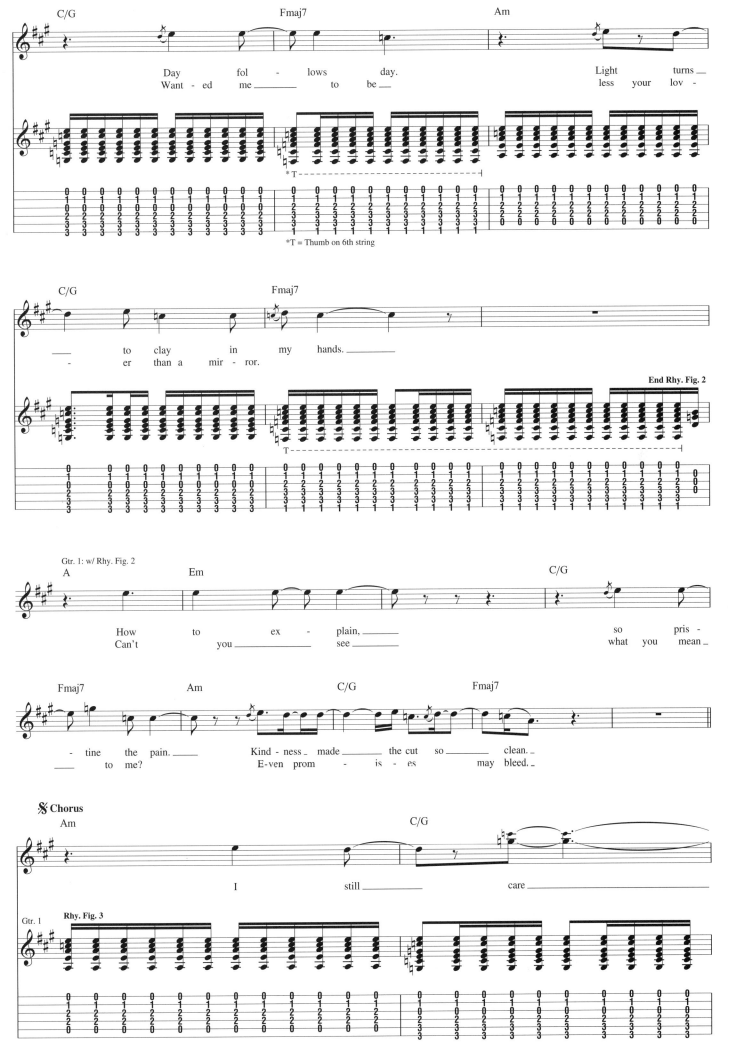

*T = Thumb on 6th string

Winter Birds

Words and Music by Ray LaMontagne

Drop D tuning, down 1 step:
(low to high) C-G-C-F-A-D

Intro
Moderately ♩ = 142

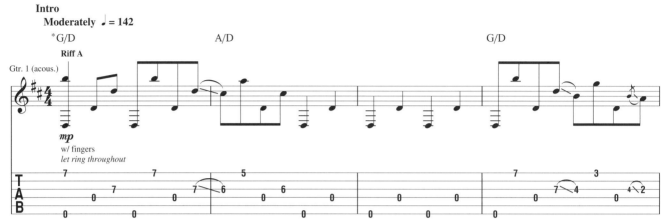

*Chord symbols reflect implied harmony.

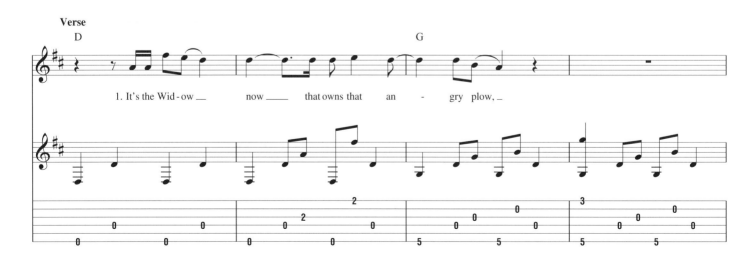

Verse

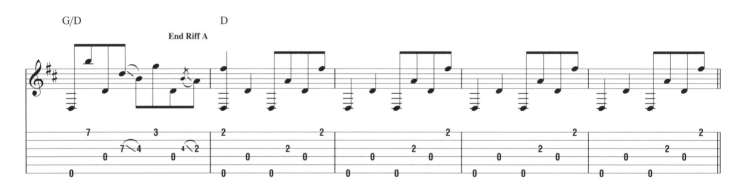

1. It's the Wid-ow __ now __ that owns that an - gry plow, _

28

Coda 1

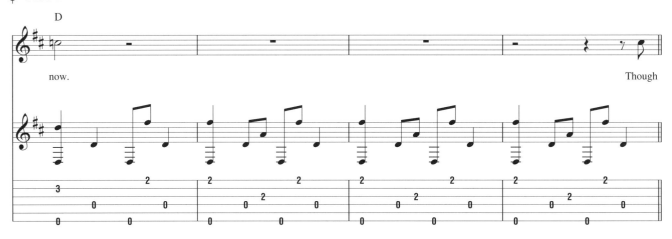

Bridge

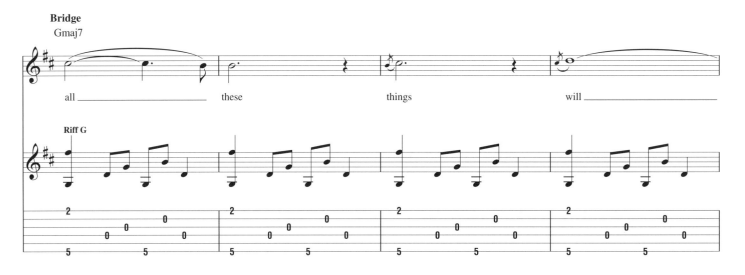

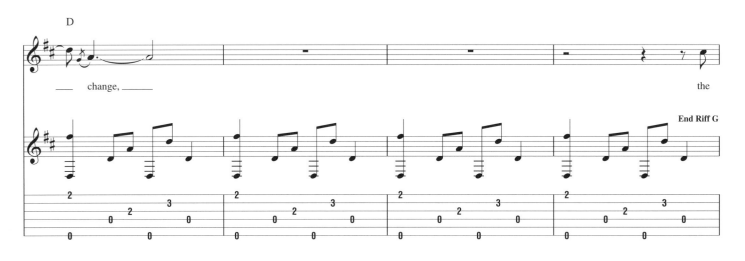

As green to gold and gold ____ to brown, ____

the leaves will __ fall _____ to feed __ the ground. ____

And in their fall - ing make no sound. __

Oh, _____ my la - dy, __ la - dy, I am lov - ing you now. ____

Interlude

Verse

4. I've gath-ered all my __ mon - ey and I'm go - in' to town

to buy _____ my la - dy a long and flow - ing gown. _

Gtr. 1: w/ Riff C

G   C

'Cause come to-mor-row morn - ing we're off to the coun - ty fair.   I'll   find   a yel-

D.S. al Coda 2

G   D

low flow - er and I will lace it in her hair. _

⊕ Coda 2

C   G   C   G5   D

Oh, _____ my la - dy, _   la - dy, I am lov-ing   you now. _

Outro

Gtr. 1: w/ Riff A

G/D   A/D   G/D   D

G/D   A/D   G/D

D   G/D

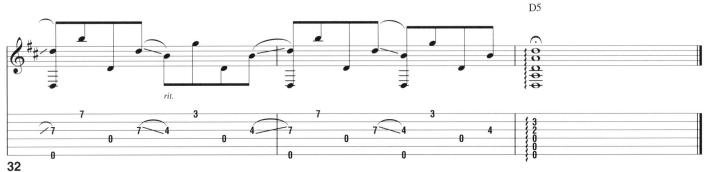

D5

rit.

Meg White

Words and Music by Ray LaMontagne

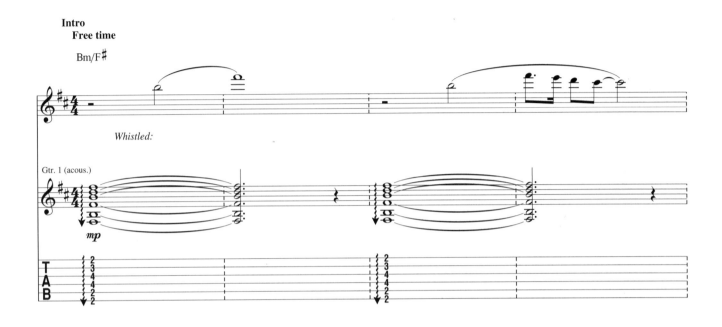

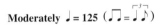

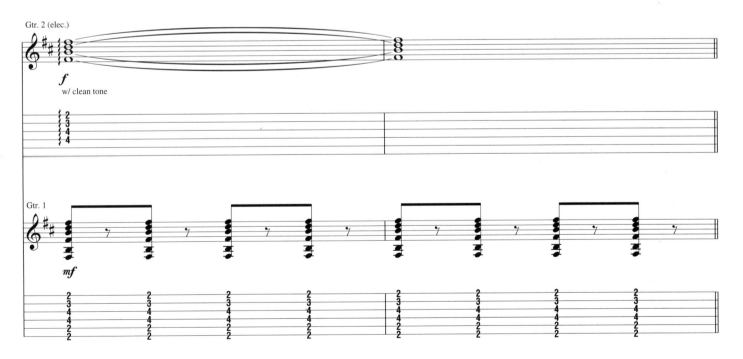

Verse

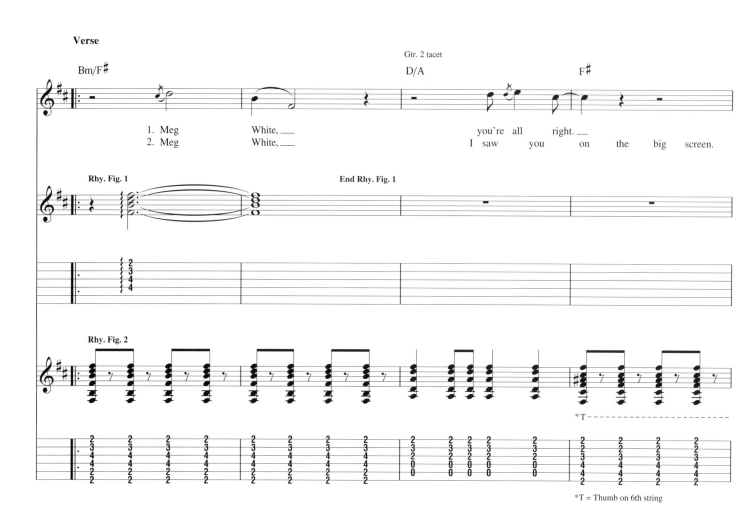

1. Meg White, ___ you're all right. ___
2. Meg White, ___ I saw you on the big screen.

*T = Thumb on 6th string

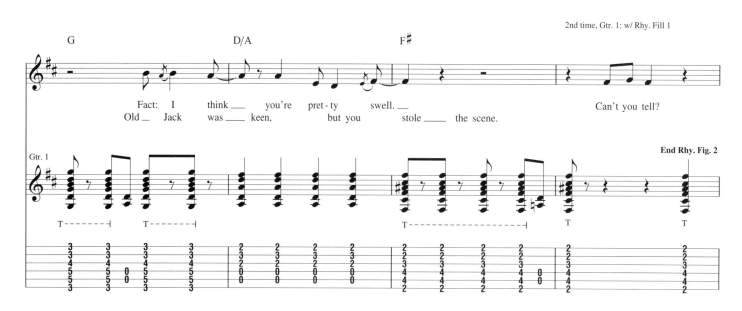

2nd time, Gtr. 1: w/ Rhy. Fill 1

Fact: I think ___ you're pret-ty swell. ___ Can't you tell?
Old ___ Jack was ___ keen, but you stole ___ the scene.

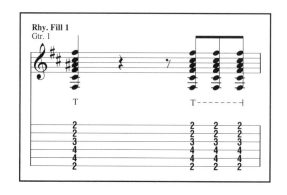

D.S. al Coda
(take 1st ending)

39

Hey Me, Hey Mama

Words and Music by Ray LaMontagne

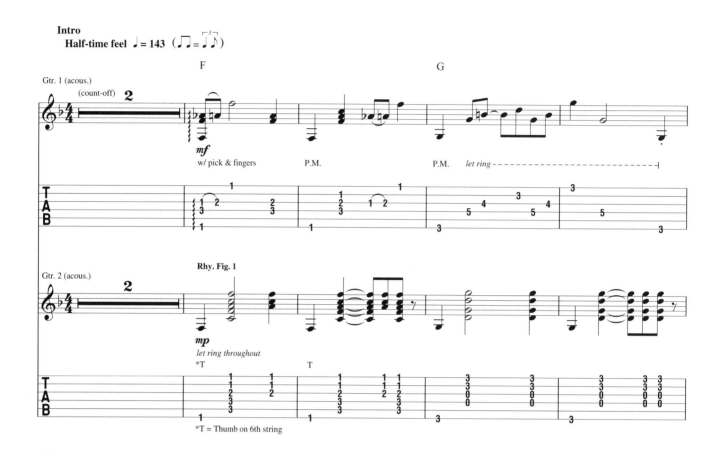

Wind sweet-ly drift-in' through that ___ rip-en-ing corn. ___
Still I would do just a-bout an-y-thing in the world ___ for you. ___ Hey me, ___
Guess I just was-n't read-y for such a heav-y hand-ed love.

Chorus

hey Ma-ma, where you been ___

for so long, ___ for so ___ long? Hey me, ___

hey Ma-ma, where you been, ___

where you   been ___   for so   long? ___

Guitar Solo

Banjo Solo

Outro-Chorus

where you been _____ for so long, _

Gtr. 1: w/ Riff A
Gtr. 2: w/ Rhy. Fig. 4

Henry Nearly Killed Me
(It's a Shame)

Words and Music by Ray LaMontagne

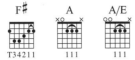

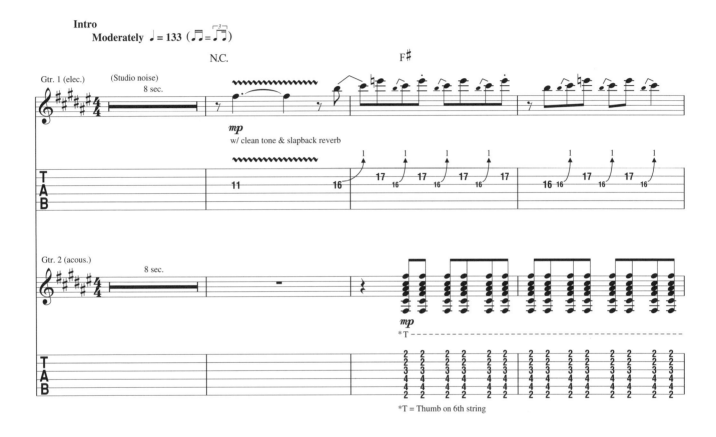

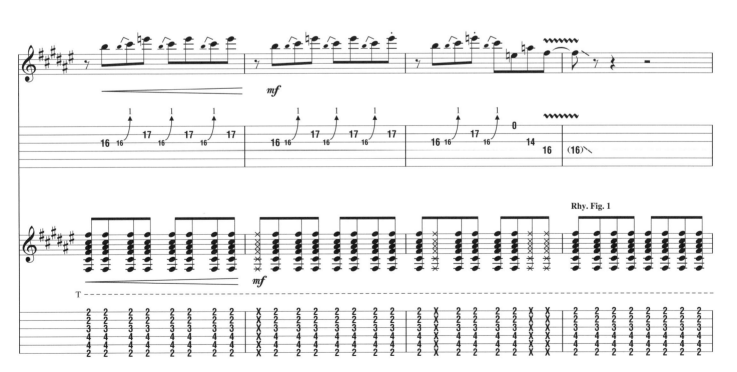

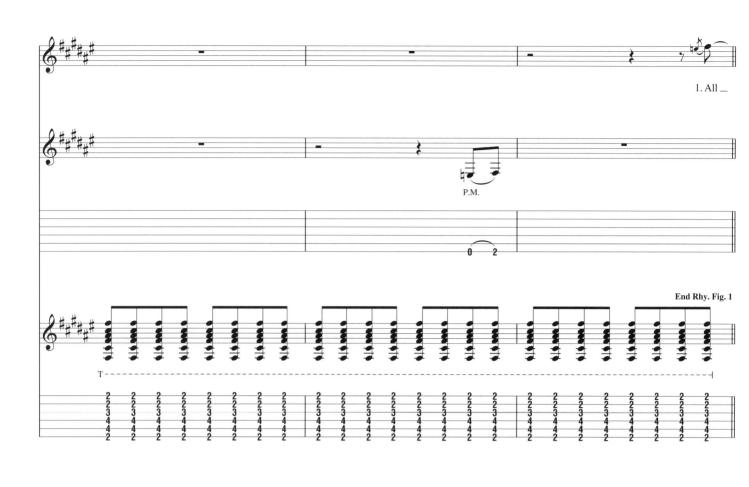

1. All __

End Rhy. Fig. 1

P.M.

Verse

Gtr. 2: w/ Rhy. Fig. 1 (4 times)

F#

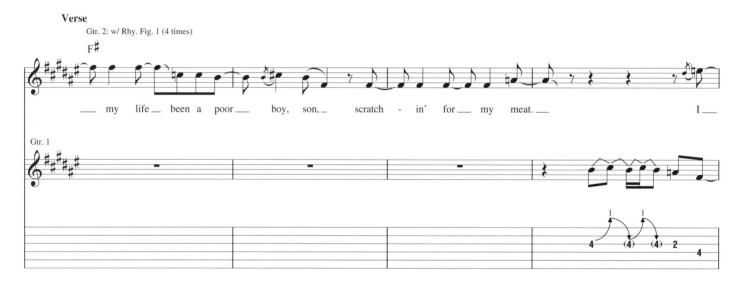

__ my life __ been a poor __ boy, son, __ scratch - in' for __ my meat. __ I __

Gtr. 1

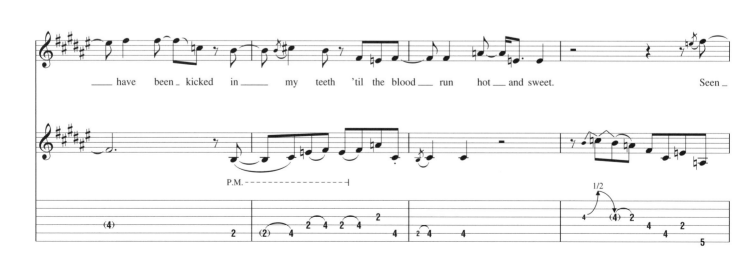

__ have been _ kicked in __ my teeth 'til the blood __ run hot __ and sweet. Seen

P.M.

1/2

Interlude

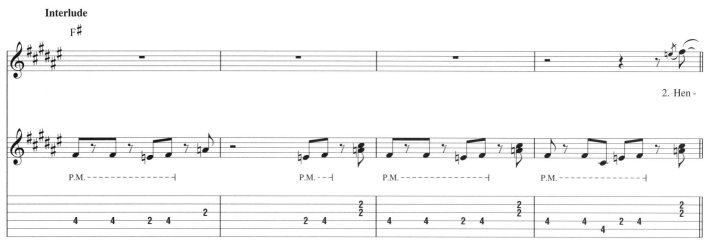

2. Hen -

Verse

-ry near-ly killed __ me 'fore they hauled __ his ass __ in jail.

Slapped __

__ me right a - cross __ my face __ with a flour __ sack full o' nails. __

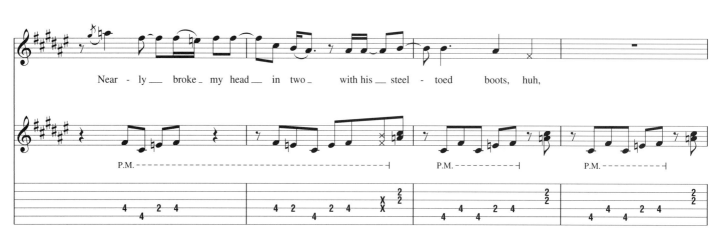

Near - ly __ broke __ my head __ in two __ with his __ steel - toed boots, huh,

eh,   eh,   mm. _____   Eh,   eh,   eh,   eh,   mm, _____   ah.

3. Sweet

_____ lit-tle Mar-y Anne ___   with her make - up all _____ in a mess,   picks

her-self up off the floor, ____ coughs, and, uh, ____ straight-ens her dress. Say-in', "Please, _

___ please, _____ Dad - dy, can I have just a bit more?" Said,

"Sor - ry, ba - by, but I'm head-in' out. Some-how this town don't feel like home an - y - more.

Hey, it's a shame, ____ shame, shame. ____ Ba - by, it's a cry -

shame, ___ shame, shame. ___ Ba - by, it's a cry - in' shame. ___

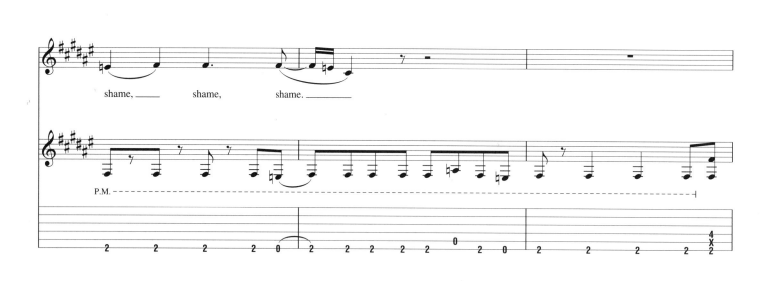

Shame, ___ shame, shame, ___ eh, eh, eh, eh, ah, ha. ____ It's a

shame, ____ shame, shame. _____

A Falling Through

Words and Music by Ray LaMontagne

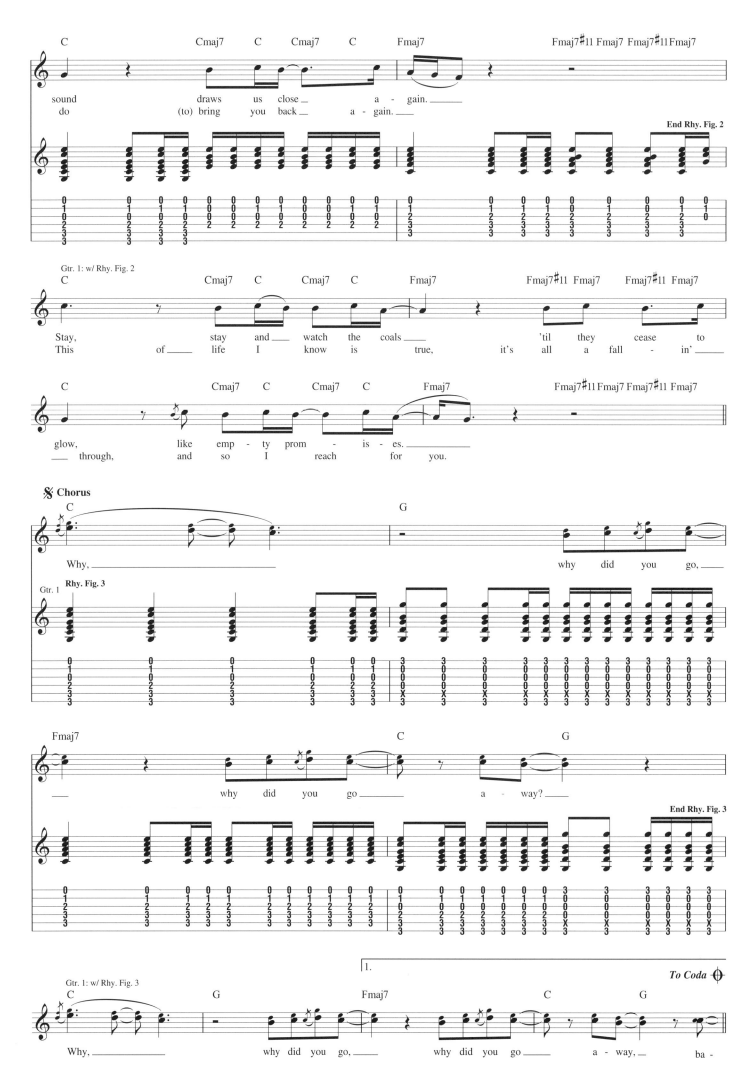

Gossip in the Grain

Words and Music by Ray LaMontagne

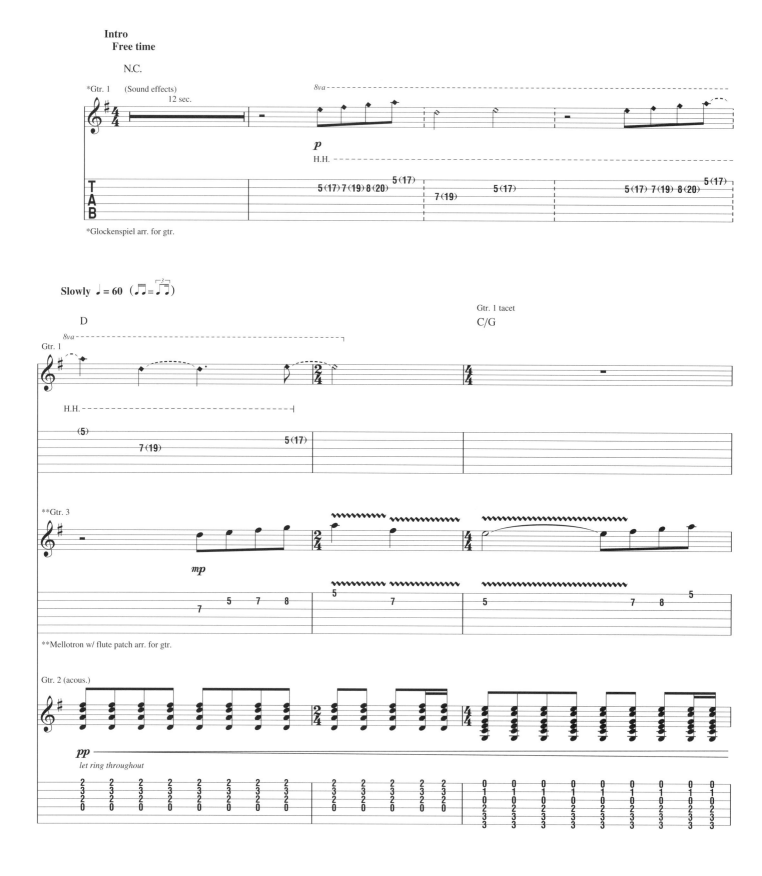

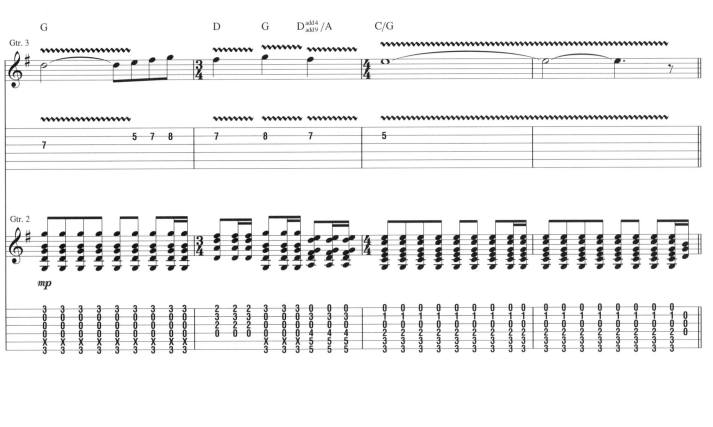

Verse

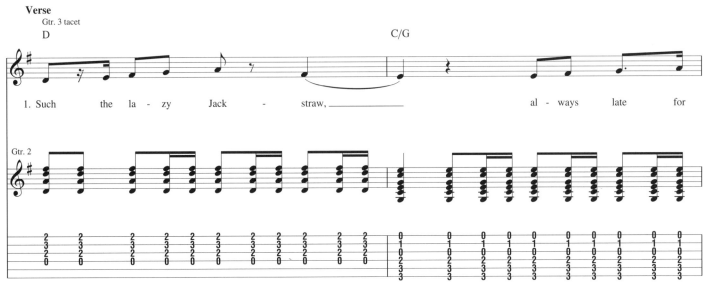

1. Such the la-zy Jack-straw, _____ al - ways late for

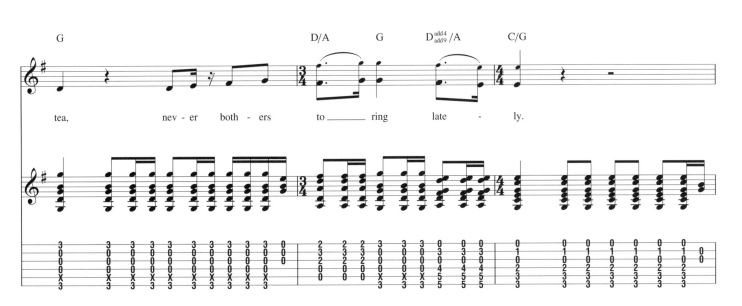

tea, nev-er both-ers to _____ ring late-ly.

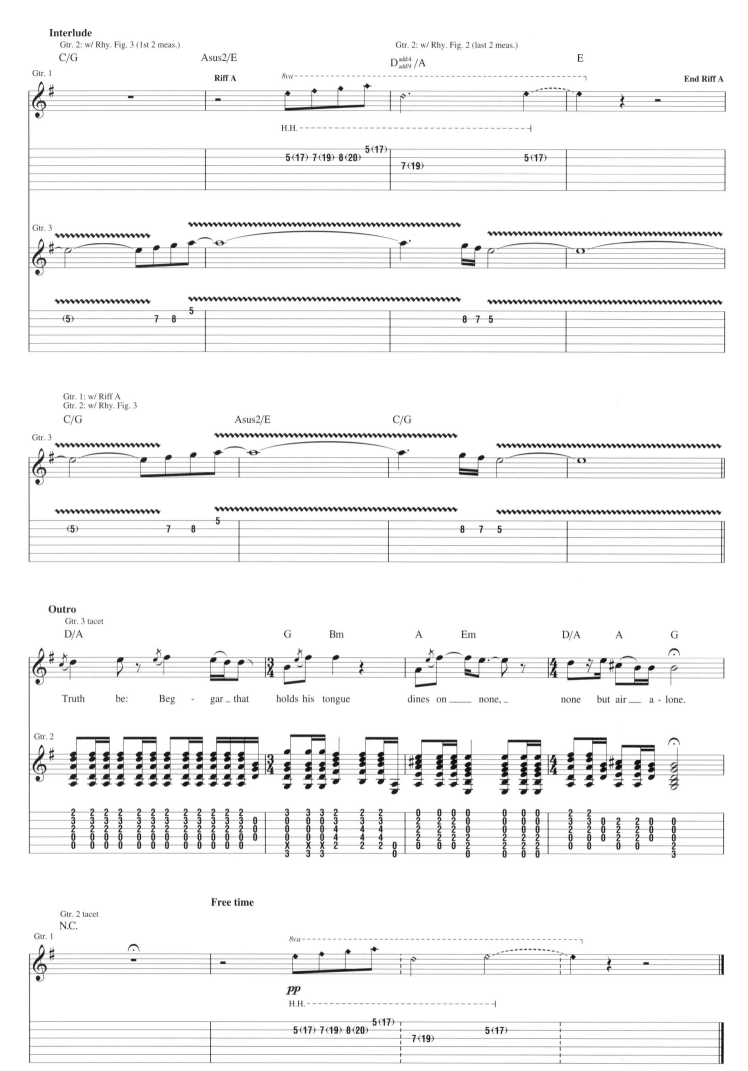